Isabella de Vito

The use of ballet in high-level rhythmic gymnastics training

Isabella de Vito

The use of ballet in high-level rhythmic gymnastics training

Study in the state of São Paulo

ScienciaScripts

Imprint

Cover image: www.ingimage.com

This book is a translation from the original published under ISBN 978-3-330-75742-4.

Publisher:
Sciencia Scripts
is a trademark of
Dodo Books Indian Ocean Ltd. and OmniScriptum S.R.L publishing group

120 High Road, East Finchley, London, N2 9ED, United Kingdom
Str. Armeneasca 28/1, office 1, Chisinau MD-2012, Republic of Moldova, Europe
Printed at: see last page
ISBN: 978-620-8-28965-2

SUMMARY

ACKNOWLEDGMENTS

I'd like to start by thanking my mother, Fâtima, because without her none of this would have been possible. She was my support, my strength and my will to keep going for four years, in the most difficult moments, she never let me give up and always encouraged me. Thank you mom for simply being my everything. I would also like to thank my stepfather, André, for his endless visits to Rio Claro, always in a good mood and always encouraging and cheering me on. I would also like to thank my siblings, Anna Claudia and André, who always supported me and lived these four years in Rio Claro with me. I would also like to thank my aunt and uncle, Ida and Ademir, my cousins, Roberta, Fernanda and Marcela, my cousins Reinaldo, Lucas and Tuco and my godmother, Mineis, for being my support in Campinas and for rescuing me several times whenever I needed it. Without them, many things would not have been possible. I would like to thank my friends in Serra Negra who never abandoned me and were always there for me, even at a distance. I couldn't forget to thank Paula, who always supported me, helped me with internships and unique opportunities within the path I chose to follow in Physical Education, part of this work is thanks to her. I would also like to thank Renata, who in this final stretch gave me the opportunity to experience something I didn't know much about and she helped me a lot.

In these four years, several people have come into my life, and many of them will be remembered for everything they have done for me. I would like to thank my advisor and friend Silvia Deutsch, who has guided and helped me at all times and has never left me helpless, in what I thought was impossible to do and today is ready. She gave me opportunities during my degree that few other students have had and I will be eternally grateful to her.

I would like to thank my sister-friends, who have been by my side since my first year and who have given me a family in Rio Claro. The ones who live with me, Thayz and Thais, for putting up with me on the hardest days and sharing everything, living together is never easy, 24 hours a day then, but I think we got through it all well and learned things on this journey that we wouldn't have learned anywhere else. The people from Rio Claro, Jessica and Cacau, who, even though we didn't live in the same house, lived like we shared the same roof, and with them we got parents and brothers who saved us and took us in whenever we needed them here in Rio Claro. I had the best experiences of college and friendship with the four of them. Friends I'll carry with me for life. I love you girls!

Thank you to the boys, Khaled, Matheus, Luiz, Leo and Henricâo, for the laughs, serious conversations and outings, never letting the routine fall by the wayside. To the guys from Tudo Nosso, especially Henrique, Renato and Danilo, for their friendship and for having come into my life in a way that will stay with me forever.

Last year, I would like to thank all the members of the 2010 Graduation Committee who spent all my Mondays until the wee hours of the morning, discussing, talking, voting, in order to put on the best graduation party, so that I could meet new people and strengthen friendships that I had only known before. I learned a lot from each of them, and from the committee in general, about how to organize parties, manage money and expenses, that asking for sponsorship isn't always easy, that publicity may not go as planned and that this isn't always a bad thing, in short, I learned things that only university couldn't teach me. Thank you to the 26 members for that.

I couldn't forget three important people who have passed through my life and enriched my knowledge of Rhythmic Gymnastics. I would like to thank Isa for all the opportunities at the RG extension, and for teaching me many things about children's training in these sports. To Ana Clara, for her trust and help when I took over the extension. And to Thays, for helping me over the last two years and getting the project off the ground with me, I'm sure the project and my girls will be in good hands with them.

I would like to thank my greatest apprentices, my students who have always trusted me and never abandoned me, with whom I found myself in the profession and one of the hardest things will be to miss the training sessions on Tuesdays and Thursdays, without talking to them, without hearing the complaints at each exercise, but in the end, to see the satisfaction and joy at each performance.

Last but not least, I would like to thank my friends who have been there for me in many ways: Pedrâo, Renato, Màrcio and Kauan, who has been a great friend for two years. And to those who have just arrived and left their mark, Bruno, Mobral, Pato, Tiagâo, Caramujo, Chico, Nicholas, Neymar and Eric. Living with the 1st year this last semester has been wonderful and unforgettable.

Thank you to everyone who took part in my achievement!

I've had the time of my life!

SUMMARY

Among the many definitions of rhythmic gymnastics, we can present it as an art and as a sport. As an art, it is conceptualized as the search for beauty, an explosion of talent and creativity, in which bodily expression and technical virtuosity develop together, forming a harmonious whole of movement and rhythm. As a sport, it is essentially a female sport, which requires a high level of development of certain physical qualities, with high performance requirements, aiming for technical perfection in the execution of complex movements with the body and apparatus.

Key words: Ballet, training, Rhythmic Gymnastics, Ballet methods

1 INTRODUCTION

Rhythmic gymnastics is essentially a women's sport and has been presented at the Olympics since 1984. It is based on dance movements and consists only of floor sequences performed on small apparatus.

According to Laffranchi (2001), as an art, Rhythmic Gymnastics is conceptualized as a search for beauty, an explosion of talent and creativity, in which bodily expression and technical virtuosity develop together, forming a harmonious set of movement and rhythm. As a sport, Rhythmic Gymnastics is essentially a female sport, which requires a high level of development of certain physical qualities, with high performance requirements, aiming for technical perfection in the execution of complex movements with the body and apparatus.

In its technical structure, Rhythmic Gymnastics is made up of the following groups of movements:

COMPULSORY BODY GROUPS (DIFFICULTIES)	OTHER C0RP0RAL GROUPS (CONNECTION ELEMENTS.DISPLACEMENTS)
*SALT0S	'VARIED DISPLACEMENTS
EQUILIBRIES	-SALTITES
'PIVOTS	-BALANCES AND CIRCUMVENTIONS
'FLEXIBILITYZONDAS	'GLROS

In addition to the body movements, the movement skills of each apparatus, which are the rope, the hoop, the float, the apples and the ribbon, are also added.

Much is said about the importance of the gymnast's posture during their performances, and it is also known that this posture is evaluated during a rhythmic gymnastics competition, but this posture does not come from a technique trained specifically in rhythmic gymnastics. Dancers develop this posture, so ballet is used to train gymnasts.

Since its beginnings in Italy, ballet has spread through various methods. Each method has its own specificity, i.e. each method emphasizes different areas of the body in its training. The basic principles of ballet are: upright posture; use of *en dehors* (external rotation of the lower limbs); body verticality; and symmetry. The best known methods today are: the Italian method, also known as the Cecchetti method; the Russian method, also known as the Vaganova method; the French method; and the English method, the famous Royal Academy of Dance.

1.1 Objectives

The aim of this study was to find out whether ballet is used in high-level Rhythmic Gymnastics training. Which ballet method is most used in Rhythmic Gymnastics, and to relate the ballet methods used with results in state/national championships.

1.2 Methods

To carry out the study, we first reviewed the literature in order to deepen our knowledge of the various ballet methods. We then surveyed several high-level rhythmic gymnastics teams in the state of Sao Paulo, who were willing to answer a questionnaire designed for this study, with the aim of verifying the use of ballet in the training of these teams. From this questionnaire, the answers obtained about the use of ballet, and which method in training, were analyzed to find out if there is a more effective one.

The questionnaire was answered by coaches from the state of Sao Paulo with an average of 11 years' experience, with the most experienced having 24 years as a coach and the youngest having 3 years' experience. Only one coach did not have a degree in Physical Education, all had a degree with specialization, but only one coach had specialization in Rhythmic Gymnastics. 80% of the coaches have teams in all categories, and only 20% do not have a team competing in pre-children's competitions.

2. LITERATURE REVIEW

2.1 Rhythmic Gymnastics

2.1.1 What it is

Rhythmic Gymnastics is a branch of gymnastics that has infinite possibilities of body movements combined with elements of ballet and theatrical dance, performed fluently in harmony with the music and coordinated with the handling of the apparatus specific to this Olympic discipline, which are the rope, the hoop, the ball, the maces and the ribbon. Only practiced by women at competition level, it also has a men's practice that originated in Japan. It has been an Olympic sport since 1984.

2.1.2 History

Rhythmic Gymnastics is a recent sport that began after the First World War, even without specific rules, when gymnastics schools began to add music and new exercises to Artistic Gymnastics, and because of the addition of these new elements, in 1946, in the Soviet Union, the sport came to be called Rhythmic Gymnastics.

According to Pallarés (1983), Rhythmic Gymnastics was systematized at the beginning of our century by Rudolfo Bode, and arose from the influence of various personalities who stood out in different branches of human culture and belonged to those who, by implementing their new ideas, gave rise to a transformation that characterized the passage from the 19th to the 20th century.

With the initial aim of educating women to develop grace, harmony of form, sensitivity and delicacy, GR was transformed over the course of the 20th century into a sport whose movements can be characterized by a complex level of difficulty. The technical details of great physical and expressive demand, systematized in the official rules of this sport today, show us the distance that we can see today between the current objectives and the initial predominantly formative objectives (Rossete, 1997). However, despite the current characterization of GR, which is quite different from what was called modern gymnastics in the first half of the 20th century, we can see that the aesthetic component is still very present and decisively interferes in the recognition of this sport on the national and world sports scene.

Several Eastern European countries organized an international championship in 1961, and the following year, the International Gymnastics Federation recognized the new sport in its rules, and the first world championship was held in 1963. Apart from the ribbon and the mallets, all the apparatuses were introduced at this championship.

The sport became Olympic in 1984, at the Los Angeles Games, when it was recognized by the IOC. And in 1996, the group event was introduced at the Olympic Games.

2.1.3 Body Elements

The body elements are the indispensable basis of the individual and joint exercises, which can be performed in different directions, planes, with or without movement, on one or two feet and coordinated with movements of the whole body. The following body elements are compulsory: walking, running, jumping, hopping, balancing, circling, turning, balancing, undulating, throwing and recovering, and the exercises must be accompanied by music. Perfect posture and execution of these elements can easily be found in ballet.

2.1.4 Training

The work of Rhythmic Gymnastics is initially based on six basic forms of movement: springing, pushing, walking, running, jumping and leaping. These have dynamic characteristics such as throwing, parrying, bouncing, hitting, walking, swinging, rolling and running.

According to Pereira (1999), rhythmic gymnastics develops physical qualities that are directly involved with the movements of the sport and that need to be worked on, such as:

Speed: A particular physical quality of the muscles and neuro-muscular coordination that allows the execution of a rapid succession of gestures that constitute, in the same action, a maximum intensity of brief or very brief duration. (Tubino, 1979, p.180)

Force: Action that causes a change in the state of motion of an object. It is the product of an object's mass and its linear acceleration. Force is measured in newtons (N). From a physiological point of view, force is the ability to exert tension against resistance, which occurs through different muscular actions. (Barbanti, 1994, p.130)

Balance: Combination of muscular actions with the purpose of assuming and supporting the body on a base, against the law of gravity. (Tubino, op. Cit., p.180)

Coordination: Integration of the central nervous system and skeletal muscles in a movement or sequence of movements (Barbanti op. cit., p.62). It allows the individual to assume awareness and execution, leading to optimum action by the various muscle groups in carrying out a sequence of movements, with maximum efficiency and economy. (Idem, p.180)

Rhythm: Physical quality explained by a chain of time, a change of tension and rest, in short, a regular variation with periodic repetitions (Idem, p.180). It is the fluency of movements in rhythmic repetitions that form part of a set of movements (Marins and Giannichi, 1996, p.111). It is order and proportion in time and space (Pallarés, 1983, p.23).

Agility: Quality of executing quick, light movements with changes of direction (Barbanti, 1994, p.07)

Endurance: The ability to sustain a workload for as long as possible without fatigue. It is also the ability of human beings to resist the fatigue that occurs during physical stress until the end of a task and, in some cases, until exhaustion (Barbanti, op.cit., p.256).

Flexibility: Voluntary execution of a movement of maximum angular amplitude, by a joint or set of joints, within morphological limits, without the risk of causing injury (Dantas, 1999, p.57).

Relaxation: A neuro-muscular phenomenon resulting from a reduction in tension in the skeletal muscles (Tubino, 1979, p.181).

Generally speaking, rhythmic gymnastics has three characteristics for practitioners to work on: body movements, the handling of apparatus and musical accompaniment. These three elements together form the unity that underpins this discipline. In practice, its training is based on direct command, which aims to repeat tasks, and on teaching and learning, through which the gymnast would know and identify the logic of her movement. As preparation, the gymnast begins physical exercises in childhood, to encourage her growth and also her social interaction, as well as improving her motor coordination, in addition to the pleasure and stimulation that comes from practicing. This preparation is done with a view to the future, in which the athlete will have improved her physical fitness and will enjoy the experiences that come from being part of a team, as well as a greater psychological structure when she has to face opposing situations, such as victory and defeat. Contrary to what you might think, physical training is only harmful when it is poorly accompanied and combined with a bad diet.

The component parts of the GRD lesson plan should be arranged as follows: introduction, educational and/or formative part, applied part and closing (Érica Saur, n.d., p.31)

Lessons should establish a chain of continuity and progression between them, and should not be a single, isolated element. Each lesson is a link in a chain of successive events, i.e. the continuation of a previous lesson and, at the same time, the start of the next lesson (Sissi Martins, 1999, p.34).

2.1.5 Scoring Code

All official rhythmic competitions are regulated by the International Gymnastics Federation, which goes by the acronym FIG. It sets the rules and calendars for all international events. National competitions are generally regulated by the various local federations. The FIG also has responsibility for the Scoring Code, the publication that guides gymnasts, coaches and referees in the preparation, composition and evaluation of the series in all events, and which also governs the results of the sport. The Scoring Code determines the competitions, juries, faults, distribution of marks, exit from the practicum, rules and controls of the apparatus, reserve apparatus, losses and recoveries, broken apparatus, apparatus contact with the ceiling, apparatus caught in the ceiling beams, reserve gymnasts, gymnasts' attire, repetition of exercises, body elements, execution, composition requirements and body difficulties. The scoring code changes with each Olympic cycle, making the sport increasingly difficult and complex (Sissi Martins, 1999).

2.2 Ballet

2.2.1 Origin

Since the origins of societies, it has been through dance and song that man has asserted himself as a member of a community (GARAUDY, 1980).

Classical *ballet* is the development and transformation of primitive dance, which was based on instinct, into a dance made up of different steps, links, gestures and figures previously elaborated for one or more participants (DI DONATO, 1994).

Ballet has its roots in Renaissance Italy through the pantomimes (plays without lines, using only facial and body expressions, usually improvised) that were performed by actors and circus performers in large halls for members of the court.

The marriage of the Italian Catherine de Medici to King Henry II of France in 1533 gave an important boost to the development of ballet. A number of artists specializing in large, lavish shows were brought over from Italy. In 1581 Catherine de Medici produced the *Ballet Comique de la Reine* in Paris under the direction of the Italian musician Baldassarino de Belgiojoso or Balthazar de

Beaujoyeulx, the name he adopted in France. The ballet took on the form in which it is known today in France during the reign of Louis XIII. In 1661, his son Louis XIV founded the *Académie de Musique et de Danse*, with the aim of systematizing, preserving quality and overseeing the teaching and production of ballet. Louis XIV appointed Charles Louis Pierre de Beauchamps to head the institution, which was dissolved in 1780.

According to Vicentim (2004), the so-called repertory ballets are based on musical compositions that helped make it popular in Europe and then in the rest of the world. Some of the most notable ballets are: Coppélia by Léo Delibes, The Firebird by Igor Stravinsky, The Nutcracker by Marius Petipa and Swan Lake by Marius Petipa and Lev Ivanov, both with music by Tchaikovsky.

From Romanticism onwards, women began to stand out and contribute to the improvement of the art. Marie Camargo, for example, created the jeté, the pas de basque and the entrechat quatre, as well as shortening dresses to above the ankles and wearing shoes without heels.

2.2.2 Ballet Methods

The techniques of ballet are based on the principles of good posture and body positioning, maintaining them throughout all the movements. The positions and movements performed in classical ballet require adequate physical preparation, good cardiac and respiratory conditioning, since the dancer can remain on stage for up to an hour and a half, depending on the choreography presented (Margherita, 1994).

The five basic foot positions in ballet require maximum external rotation of the hips, which helps the dancers to execute graceful and aesthetic movements. These positions are considered basic and are divided from the first to the fifth position, in this sequence, all of which should promote a rotation in which the feet are positioned at 180°. There are also twenty-six positions for the lower limbs, seven for the torso and seven for the arms, which are performed with the feet fully on the ground, in mid-point plantar flexion, with the knees extended or at the tips. Therefore, there is a huge possibility of variations that can be performed in CCF and CCA (Bertoni, 1992; Margherita, 1994; Khan et al, 1995).

As a result, ballet schools have sprung up in various countries such as Italy, Russia, England, France and Cuba, emphasizing different ballet techniques.

2.2.3 Vaganova method

This method is derived from the teachings of Agripina Vaganova, a Russian ballerina who dedicated herself to teaching ballet when she retired from the stage. She created the book "The basic principles of classical ballet", based on the work of several teachers from the Leningrad Choreographic School, emphasizing gradual learning through the student's body awareness of each movement.

In this method, the exercises are not set as in RAD. According to the guidelines given, each teacher choreographs their own class and the students dance it in their exams. The instructions for the teachers are precise, leading to attention to detail and precision of movement. Their work is mainly focused on developing the characteristics needed for dancers to be able to perform *Pas de Deux*, and special emphasis is placed on dancing with the whole body rather than simply executing movements mechanically.

In the Vaganova method, unlike the Cecchetti method, where the hands flow invisibly from one position to another, the hands are given greater attention, energy and power, leaving them behind and bringing them back at the last moment.

The first stages focus on *epaulement* and the stability and strength of the back, aiming for a fluid and harmonious movement. While working on technique, art is also acquired individually, providing a strong and melodious expressiveness. The Vaganova method emerged in the midst of the issues arising from the Russian Revolution at the beginning of the 20th century and resulted in a change in the way ballet was viewed in Russia.

This method is taught massively in Russia and has become popular and widely adopted in Europe, North America and other regions. Mikhail Baryshnikov was a dancer trained using the Vaganova method.

2.2.4 Cecchetti Method

Enrico Cecchetti was the great master of the Cecchetti technique, through the

Cecchetti Society. He was one of the greatest ballet teachers ever known. He created a teaching system that would justify the success of many students, with a complex and elaborate lesson plan to train dancers for professional work.

Its rigorous formula produces dancers with the strength, balance, elasticity and poise needed for difficult steps and turns. In this method, students undergo demanding training dedicated to shaping and preparing their bodies for any choreographic requirement they are presented with. A notable emphasis is placed on the fluency of the arms when moving from one position to another, much more so than in any other method.

The structure of the method is based mainly on repeating sets of exercises to which one day of each week is dedicated. Cecchetti also stressed that in addition to these exercises, the teacher should add sequences of steps each day that he or she has composed so that the students learn to assimilate new sequences quickly. The steps are started on one side of the leg one week and on the opposite side the next, alternately, so that the students think of the movement of the body as a whole and not just of each part of the body separately, which serves to enhance the concept of the line of the body and of movement.

To this day, 40 stages are used in the step sequences exactly as Enrico Cecchetti wrote them, aiming for balance in each leg, well-aligned posture and the gracefulness developed by his *por de Bràs* exercises. However, for all its science and unalterability, the Cecchetti method is criticized for its monotony and accused of not keeping the student's interest, and the teachers counter this criticism by saying that the student is not in class to have fun, but to learn their trade.

In Cecchetti's hands have passed great dancers such as Anna Pavlova, Pierina Lengnani, Vaslav Nijinsky, George Balanchine, Michael Fokine and the dancers of Sergei Diaghilev's company.

The method was codified and transcribed by dance historian Cyril Beaumont, supervised by Stanislav Idzikovski and Cecchetti himself, under the name "The Manual of the Theory and Practice of Classical Theatrical Dancing(Cecchetti Method)".

Better known as the Italian Method, the Cecchetti method is little known in Brazil.

2.2.5 Royal Academy Of Dance

It is certainly the most popular system in Brazil. Its technique has been developed in such a way as to be well disseminated in its Syllabus, i.e. the subject is passed on to the student in such a way that they don't feel pressured to learn. He works a lot on lines, taking special care with children and young dancers. The Royal method believes in the importance of each student, offering them a challenge to demonstrate their understanding and knowledge of the work. This method for exams (Syllabus) has been carefully designed:

*Clearly defined and differentiated objectives for each level.

*A global plan indicating the stages of evolution

*The scaling of marks given for the various degrees of skill.

2.2.6 French Method

Probably the oldest of the methods. He is credited with the creation of classical technique, so much so that the vast majority of ballet steps are in French. Its most famous creator is Pierre Blauchamp, who collected and codified the positions of the feet and arms. It is perhaps the most rigid ballet method.

2.2.7 Training

Correct ballet training begins on the barre. According to Cosentino (1985), the barre serves as a support for the execution of the exercises that will give the dancers security, support, lightness, adequate musculature and knowledge of the other steps and technical movements. After the barre exercises, the center exercises begin, where exercises are performed based on the activities already done on the barre, but without its help, with the aim of improving the dancer's balance. The final part of the class is the *port de bras*, which are arm movements combined with head and back movements, without forgetting breathing, which must be worked on with harmony and awareness. And as if it were a farewell, there is a series of movements called reverences.

According to Schafle (1996), intermediate level dancers attend classes 3 to 5 times a week and the intensity levels are increased. Still according to Schafle (1996, apud Simas and Guimarâes 2002), girls begin to work on their toes and both sexes begin to increase the height and complexity of their jumps and turns, as well as performing more advanced attitudes or balancing positions. As the level of skill increases, the frequency of classes also increases and may include summer sessions with unfamiliar teachers and longer dance days than usual. Consequently, attempts to increase external rotation (*en dehors*) and flexibility may increase out of proportion to the student's level of skill.

At the advanced levels, the introduction of tiptoe work is the first stage in separating serious dancers from those who want to, or may be able to, dance only for recreational purposes. From the first class onwards, the barre and center exercises in *ballet* are designed to strengthen the feet and lower extremity in preparation for tiptoe work. Strength and level of technique should be the criteria for deciding when it is possible to dance on tiptoe (SCHAFLE, 1996).

It is very important to teach the technique of using a high-top shoe, and it is the teacher's duty to know when the child should start using the shoe, which should not only be at the right age, but also according to the child's maturity (HANKIN, 1997).

According to Simas and Guimaraes (2002), in this way, body image ends up being part of the classical ballet routine - support, balance, pointe shoes - and a slim body is a constant in the dancer's life, even though there is no scientific evidence that it is necessary to be slim in order to dance.

2.2.8 Benefits of Rhythmic Gymnastics

According to Laffranchi (2001), as an art, Rhythmic Gymnastics is conceptualized as a search for beauty, an explosion of talent and creativity, in which body expression and technical virtuosity develop together, forming a harmonious set of movement and rhythm. As a sport, Rhythmic Gymnastics is essentially a female sport, which requires a high level of development of certain physical qualities, with high performance requirements, aiming for technical perfection in the execution of complex movements with the body and apparatus. According to Pereira (1999), rhythmic gymnastics develops physical qualities that are directly involved with the movements of the sport and that need to be worked on, such as speed, strength, balance, coordination, rhythm, agility, endurance, flexibility and relaxation.

According to Simas and Guimaraes (2002) "the practice of classical *ballet* makes it possible to develop and enrich the qualities of man, and in this context Achcar (1998) says that bodily beauty, vision, precision, coordination, flexibility, tenacity, imagination and expression are the essence of *ballet* teaching."

Comparing the ideas of Laffranchi, Achcar and Pereira, both practices require beauty/body expression, virtuosity, flexibility, coordination and rhythm. So we can say that ballet helps rhythmic gymnastics and vice versa.

3. RESULTS AND DISCUSSION

The results were analyzed descriptively.

The number of coaches who have been gymnasts in this sport can be seen in Graph 1.

Graph 1: Frequency of "yes" and "no" answers to the question: Have you ever been a gymnast?

The number of techniques that were familiar with ballet methods can be seen in graph 2.

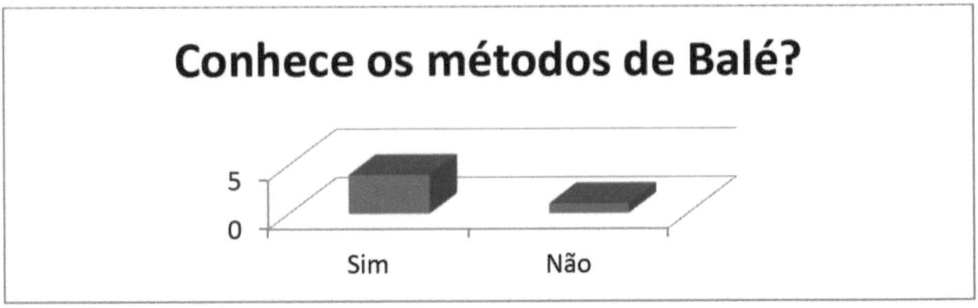

Graph 2: Frequency of "yes" and "no" answers to the question: Are you familiar with ballet methods?

The ballet methods known by the techniques can be seen in chart 3.

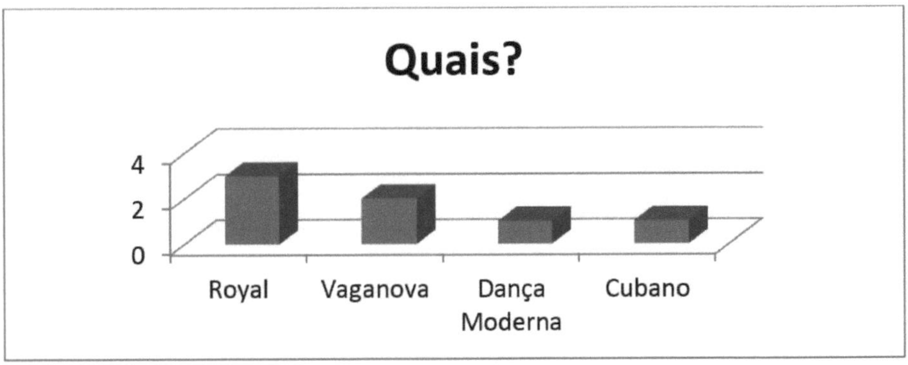

Graph 3: Ballet methods mentioned by the techniques.

The number of techniques that have already practiced ballet can be seen in graph 4.

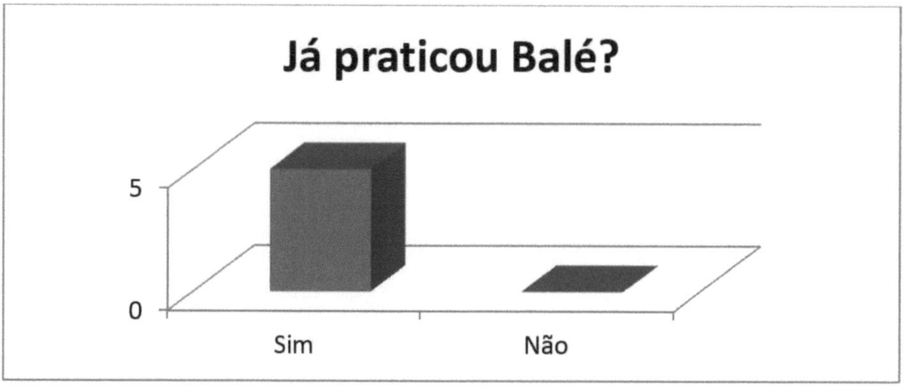

Graph 4: Frequency of "yes" and "no" answers to the question: Have you ever practiced ballet?

The number of techniques practiced during Rhythmic Gymnastics training can be seen in Graph 5.

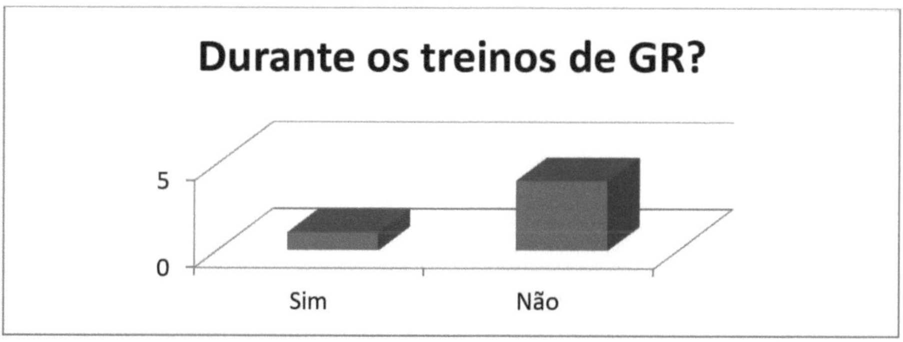

Graph 5: Frequency of "yes" and "no" answers to the question: Did you practice ballet during your GR training?

The number of techniques that think ballet is important for Rhythmic Gymnastics can be seen in Graph 6.

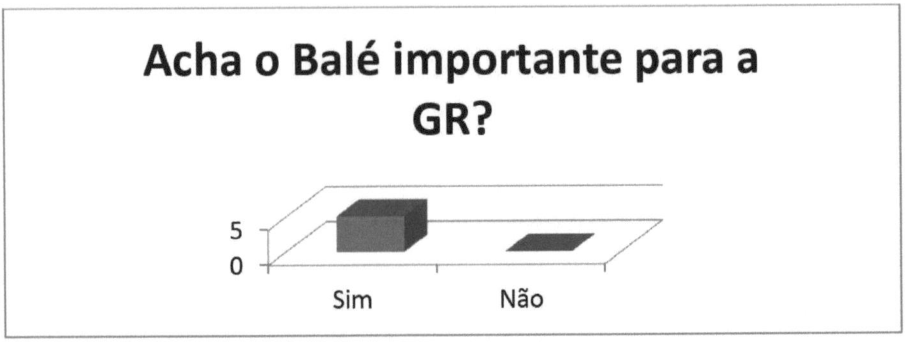

Graph 6: Frequency of "yes" and "no" answers to the question: Do you think ballet is important for rhythmic gymnastics?

The number of techniques that use ballet in Rhythmic Gymnastics training can be seen in Graph 7.

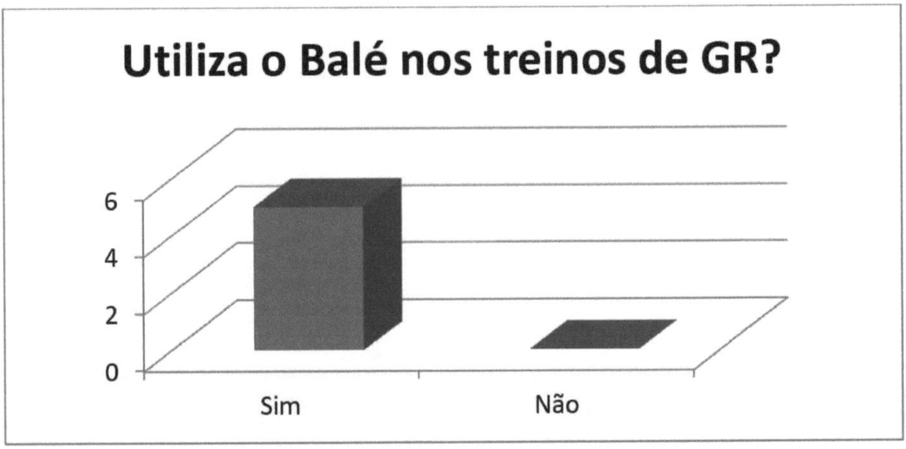

Graph 7: Frequency of "yes" and "no" answers to the question: Do you use ballet in your Rhythmic Gymnastics training?

The ballet methods used by the techniques can be seen in graph 8.

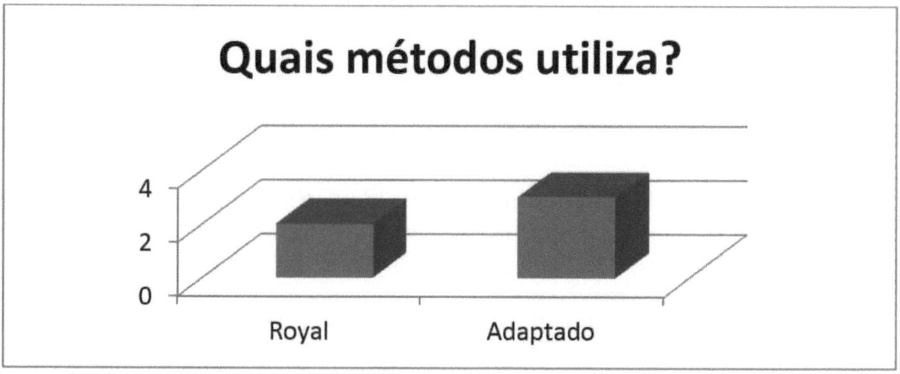

Graph 8: Ballet methods used by techniques.

The number of techniques that use physical training in Rhythmic Gymnastics training can be seen in graph 9.

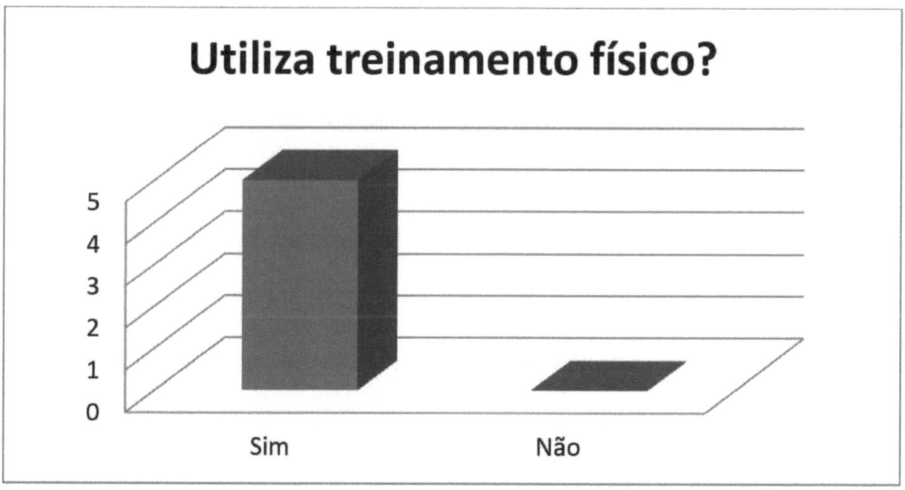

Graph 9: Frequency of "yes" and "no" answers to the question: Do you use physical training during your Rhythmic Gymnastics workouts?

Of all the techniques, 80% had been gymnasts, and only one didn't know ballet methods. Of those who did, the methods mentioned were: Royal Academy of Dance, Vaganova, Cuban Ballet and Modern Dance. All the coaches have practiced ballet, think it is important for Rhythmic Gymnastics and use ballet in their training. Among the methods used, the most frequently cited were those adapted to Rhythmic Gymnastics and the Royal Academy. However, only 20% of the coaches used ballet in their Rhythmic Gymnastics training when they were gymnasts. All the techniques use physical training during their workouts.

According to Cosentino (1985), the barre serves as a support for the execution of the exercises that will give the dancers security, support, lightness, adequate musculature and knowledge of the other steps and technical movements. After the barre exercises, the center exercises begin, where exercises are performed based on the activities already done on the barre, but without its help, with the aim of improving the dancer's balance. The final part of the class is the *port de bras*, which are arm movements combined with head and back movements, without forgetting breathing, which must be worked on with harmony and awareness. And as if it were a farewell, there is a series of movements called reverences. All of this is necessary in Rhythmic Gymnastics, which proves that ballet is useful in this discipline.

According to Alarcón J. (1997), classical dance, due to its technical characteristics and class structure with exercises designed and experienced by many generations of dancers, offers Rhythmic Gymnastics a wide range of exercises for the gymnast's technical preparation.

Bar work and exercises to prepare for jumps, poses and strides, as well as flexibility and range of movement, are of great importance in preparing the fundamental groups of body elements required in the CFIG. (ALARCÓN J. 1997, p.62)

According to Schwabowski *et all* (1992), classical dance in general contributes to the gymnast's preparation:

- External rotation of the legs

- Postural education and body tensioning

- Coordination and rhythm

- Coordination of head with arms and legs

- Rhythm awareness

- Specific strength and mobility combined with coordination

Rhythmic Gymnastics training should include the bar and center exercises of this style for the best specific development of the physical abilities needed to learn the body elements. These abilities are the power and rapid strength of the leg segment, flexibility of the trunk, amplitude of the leg and arm segments, active and passive flexibility, balance capacity for postures, agility and general and specific anaerobic endurance.

However, no study on ballet in Rhythmic Gymnastics specifically can be found in the literature, thus lacking more information.

4. CONCLUSION

Among the most cited ballet methods was the Royal Academy of Dance. This may be due to the fact that it is the most widespread method in Brazil. Another reason for its greater use may be that it was adapted to Rhythmic Gymnastics by former Brazilian national team coach Barbara Lafrancchi. This has made it known in this area for its influential techniques in this sport. So, based on this research, we can't say which method is the most efficient, but we can say that ballet's efficiency in rhythmic gymnastics training is important and common among high-level teams.

This shows that it is important to publicize existing ballet methods more widely and to spread the word about their importance in the technical preparation of gymnasts.

Due to the small number of participants, the results of the research do not show the complete picture of Brazilian rhythmic gymnastics, but we have been able to reflect on the technical preparation of our gymnasts. It is clear that in rhythmic gymnastics performances the presence of ballet is of fundamental importance. It remains to be seen what level of knowledge our coaches should have in order to be able to develop it with their gymnasts.

5. BIBLIOGRAPHICAL REFERENCES

Ballet: History. Available at: http://pt.wikipedia.org/wiki/Balé Accessed on: 11/03/2010 at 16:41.32

Ballet. Available at:

http://www.escoladedanca.net/course/category.php?id=5 Accessed on: 28/10/2009 at 18:35.26

BERTONI, I.G. **A dança e a evoluçâo, o ballet e seu contexto teòrico, programaçâo didâtica**. Sâo Paulo: Temz do Brasil, 1992.

DI DONATO, S. History of dance. **Revista Dançar**, Rio de Janeiro, v. 1, p. 10, 1994.

GARAUDY, R. **Dançar a vida**. Rio de Janeiro: Nova Fronteira, 1980.

Rhythmic Gymnastics: History and Origin. Available at

http://pt.wikipedia.org/wiki/Ginàstica ritmica Accessed: 11/03/2010 at 16:34.12

HANKIN, T. Facilitating discovery: student-centered teaching strategies in the technique class. **JOPERD,** [United States], v. 68, no. 1, p. 36-38, 1997.

KHAN, K. et al. Overuse Injuries in classical ballet. **Sports Med,** v. 5, n. 19, p. 341-357, 1995.

LAFRANCCHI, B. E. **Sports Training Applied to Rhythmic Gymnastics**.

Londrina: Unopar, 2001. 157 p.

MARGHERITA, A.J. Issues in gynastics and dancers. **Sports Medicine and Rehabilitation: a sportspecific approach,** Philadelphia, p.151-167, 1994.

Cecchetti Method. Available at:

http://balletmonde.blogsome.com/2007/06/21/metodo- cecchetti/ Accessed on: 28/10/2009 at 18:40.02

Vaganova Method. Available at:

http://balletmonde.blogsome.com/2007/07/26/metodo- vaganova/ Accessed: 28/10/2009 at 18:53.47

Ballet Methods. Available at: http://meadd.com/ballerina/news/243238 Accessed on: 11/03/2010 at 16:57.02

PALLARÉS, Z. **Ginàstica Ritmica.** 2.ed. Porto Alegre, PRODIL, 1983. 206p.

PEREIRA, S.A.M. **Ginàstica Ritmica Desportiva:** Aprendendo Passo a Passo. Rio de Janeiro, Shape, 1999.

PORPINO, K.O. Training Rhythmic Gymnastics: Aesthetic Reflections. **Rev. Bras. Ciência. Esporte**, v. 26, n. 1, p. 121-133, 2004.

REYNO F, A.; ALARCON J, T. **Gimnasia Ritmica Deportiva**. Styles of Dance in Rhythmic Sports Gymnastics. Study of Body Elements. University of Playa Ancha, 1997.

SCHAFLE, M. D. **Secrets in sports medicine**: answers you need every day in training centers, in the clinic and in oral and written exams. Porto Alegre: Artes Médicas, 1996.

VICENTIM, Josiane. **Body awareness in classical ballet and contemporary dance: students' and choreographers' views.** 2004. 76f. Course Conclusion Work (Physical Education) - Biosciences Institute/Universidade Paulista, Rio Claro.

6. APPENDICES

6.1 Appendix 1 - Letter of Introduction

Invitation letter

Dear Technician,

I am a student studying for a Bachelor's degree in Physical Education at the Biosciences Institute - UNESP - Rio Claro Campus, and I would like to ask you to voluntarily participate in my research project, the subject of which is related to the use of ballet in high-level Rhythmic Gymnastics training.

The sample of this study will be made up of Rhythmic Gymnastics coaches who constantly take part in state and national competitions.

Your participation is of fundamental importance if this study is to be carried out in the best possible way. I am therefore at your disposal to answer any questions you may have. I would also like to point out that your identity will be kept confidential and data will be disclosed for research purposes only with your consent.

Sincerely,

Isabella de Vito Ribeiro Bernardino

Undergraduate student in Physical Education -

UNESP-IB-RC

6.2 Appendix 2 - Questionnaire applied to techniques

QUESTIONNAIRE

Personal Data

Name: ____________________________________

Date of birth :___/___/ ______ Tel: ( )

Sex : ( )F ( ) M

City:

Club that works: ____________________________

Há how long is the technique? _________________

Education: Degree in Physical Education ( ) Other ( )

Which one: ________________________________

Postgraduate degree: Latus Sensu ( ) Strictus Sensu ( )

Which one: ________________________________

Where:_____________________________________

Do you have a course or internship in the field in another country? ( ) Yes

( ) No

Which one: ______________________________

Where: _________________________________

____

With

who:

In which categories do you have teams? __________

Which championships did you take part in between the years of:

2007____

____

____

____

2008____

____

____

____

2009____

____

____

____

What were the rankings?

2007____

____

____

____

2008____

____

____

____

2009____

____

____

____

Specific questionnaire

1. Have you ever been a gymnast?

( )Yes ( )No

2. Do you know ballet methods?

( )Yes ( )No

Which ____

3. Have you ever practiced ballet?

( )Yes ( )No

4. If so, did you practice during your Rhythmic Gymnastics training?

( )Yes ( )No

5. Do you think ballet is important for rhythmic gymnastics?

( )Yes ( )No

Justify your answer:

6. Do you use ballet in your training?

( )Yes ( )No

7. If so, which method do you use? ____________

8. For what purpose do you use ballet?

9. Do you use physical training?

( )Yes ( )No

If so, what kind?

____

____

____

____

____

10. Any comments you'd like to make?

Thank you for answering this questionnaire! ! !

Isabella de Vito Ribeiro Bernadino

Silvia Deutsch

MIX
Papier aus verantwortungsvollen Quellen
Paper from responsible sources
FSC® C105338

Printed by Books on Demand GmbH, Norderstedt / Germany